Where there's a Will, there's a Relative

AN EXECUTOR'S GUIDE TO WILLS AND PROBATE

ROBERT STELL FCCA

Copyright © 2020 Robert Stell

The moral right of the author has been asserted.

Apart from any fair dealing for the purposes of research or private study, or criticism or review, as permitted under the Copyright, Designs and Patents Act 1988, this publication may only be reproduced, stored or transmitted, in any form or by any means, with the prior permission in writing of the publishers, or in the case of reprographic reproduction in accordance with the terms of licences issued by the Copyright Licensing Agency. Enquiries concerning reproduction outside those terms should be sent to the publishers.

Matador
9 Priory Business Park,
Wistow Road, Kibworth Beauchamp,
Leicestershire. LE8 0RX
Tel: 0116 279 2299
Email: books@troubador.co.uk
Web: www.troubador.co.uk/matador
Twitter: @matadorbooks

ISBN 978 1800463 844

British Library Cataloguing in Publication Data.
A catalogue record for this book is available from the British Library.

Printed and bound in the UK by TJ Books Limited, Padstow, Cornwall

Matador is an imprint of Troubador Publishing Ltd

CONTENTS

Foreword	5
Definition of an Executor and their duties	7
What is a Will and what does it do?	11
Sample Will	16
Intestacy	23
Flowchart outlining Intestacy Rules	24
Valuation of Assets	27
What is an Estate and what is in it?	31
Inheritance Tax	35
Trusts	39
Obtaining the Probate (Grant of Representation)	41
Settling the Estate	43
Schedule of Assets and Liabilities	47

FOREWORD

"I want everyone to leave the room, except for the cat."

If you have just been appointed as an Executor to someone's Will, this book is for you. To be an Executor of a Will does not require any legal training but it is, however, legally complex. In this book I am imagining you, the reader, as the recently appointed Executor of your grandmother's Estate. We will be looking at your role as it might be with the Will having been created and also with the Will having not been created. We will also be looking at the tasks you might wish to undertake in advance of the Estate administration as well as the many onerous tasks during the Estate administration.

Executors are also known as personal representatives and there are a maximum of four that are allowed.

So, you've just been informed by Granny Jones (aged 92) that you have been appointed as the sole Executor of her Will. You have been chosen to do this because you are the sensible one and your siblings and other relatives have spent all their lives frittering away their money. Granny Jones regards you as a solid and upstanding citizen and who will, therefore, execute her Last Will and Testament in accordance with **her** wishes. For this you may receive no reward whatsoever, except for a load of grief from said siblings and relatives. There is no law in this country that requires you to use a solicitor or even an accountant (my firm, Bradbury Stell Probate Services Limited, is licensed to carry out probate work). Although it is almost certainly easier if you do use professionals, you are not legally obliged to and it certainly won't mean you avoid any family conflict!

What I am going to do in this book is to lay out the probate process and your responsibilities in it and my advice as to how to go about this to avoid as much trouble as possible.

DEFINITION OF AN EXECUTOR AND THEIR DUTIES

So, as it happens, your favourite Granny Jones has called you up and told you that you have the honour of being appointed as the sole Executor to her Will. Your duties, as the Executor, are to literally execute what she wants to happen to all her assets and chattels after her death. You may also find that you are a beneficiary but that does not stop you being the person that executes the Will. There are all sorts of assets that Granny Jones has and in her Will she will probably have left specific instructions with regard to specific assets to specific people and then more general instructions as to what will happen to the rest of her Estate (known as the residuary Estate).

When you, the Executor, are first appointed, one of the key aspects that you will need to determine is what is going to be in Granny Jones's Estate? I'm sure in exchange for a cup of tea and some biscuits Granny Jones will happily sit you down and point to all the drawers where all the information is kept. At this stage, therefore, this is simply an exercise of making a list of all the things that Granny Jones owns. This will include investments, bank accounts, property, chattels etc. The word 'chattels' which is an ancient mediaeval term literally refers to 'all the other stuff'. Most of this stuff will be of sentimental value but not financial value but could for instance include paintings and furniture that have value. After this process of chatting to Granny Jones and making notes, a preliminary list can then be compiled and at a later date cross-checked to documents that she has. So in other words at the end of this exploratory exercise, as Executor you will aim to have a complete list of Granny Jones's assets, where the documentation for these assets is, and the value of the assets at the time of writing.

As the Executor you literally execute the Will of the Testator. The Testator is the person that has drawn up their Will. In the next chapter we will deal with the Will but for now let's assume that Granny Jones has made a Will and you are now at the stage where you have a list of her assets which you have drawn up and that can now be matched with her Will. What I mean by this is you need to make sure that the Will she has drawn up is able to be executed with the assets that you know she possesses. When I say assets, of course, that is net assets after liabilities have been deducted.

If you are happy that the Will can be executed with the means at her disposal at the time of you drawing up the schedule of assets, for now your role as the Executor is on hold.

In practical reality no-one actually knows when they are going to die! The time gap between you first being appointed Executor and the actual death of Granny Jones may be some years away. As she is 92 that is, to be blunt, probably not too distant and she is unlikely to gamble all her money away in the meantime. However, it would be wise on your part to keep in touch with Granny Jones and to make sure that you are fully up to speed with any major changes in the disposition of her assets.

So let's fast forward to the next stage which is, of course, your responsibilities upon hearing of the death of Granny Jones.

You have just been informed by your great aunt that Granny Jones has actually passed away. At this point, as the sole Executor, you must spring into action, difficult though that might be. These are the immediate steps that you should take –

- Registering the death (assuming other immediate family have not already done so)
- Arranging the funeral (as above)
- Getting a copy of the death certificate
- Securing the property and valuables to make sure they don't move… See title of book
- Informing the local authority and the utility companies
- Informing insurance companies that the property is now vacant

- Informing all pension providers (including State pension) of the death so that they stop payment. If you fail to do this all that will happen is that you will have to pay the money back to the pension companies which can be a bit of a chore to say the least

- Making sure mail is redirected

- Making sure pets are rehoused or in extreme circumstances informing RSPCA. (check expression of wishes which might give details of what the deceased wishes to happen to pets)

- Making sure that all the details of the deceased's Estate are all brought together in one place. Referring back to the original list that you had compiled with Granny Jones, it is now imperative that all those various certificates, bank accounts etc are all put together in the same place.

In this imagined scenario, it is of course highly improbable that Granny Jones has gone on a property buying spree in between appointing you as the Executor and her final demise. The likelihood is that the property she owned at the time you were appointed Executor is the property she held at death. She may, however, have opened new bank accounts or moved bank and she may have disposed of some of the specific assets that she wanted to leave to specific people in her Will. She may have moved her investments to another investment firm …… but what you, as the Executor, do have is the original list and also you do know where Granny Jones kept all these bits and pieces.

So armed with the original list, your job now is to create a final list of all of those assets and their whereabouts.

WHAT IS A WILL AND WHAT DOES IT DO?

A Will is literally a series of instructions that a person (called a Testator) leaves so that the Executor can carry out their instructions with regard to the assets and chattels that they hold on their death.

God changes his will

A Will can be drawn up by anyone, it doesn't have to be drawn up by a solicitor or a probate practitioner and Will writing kits can be obtained from Mr Google. Having been told by Granny Jones that you are the Executor, the first thing of course that you need to see is the Will. What if there hasn't been a Will? What happens if she dies without having made a Will? If Granny Jones has not made a Will, you should definitely persuade her to do that and we will come on to that shortly. If she refuses to make a Will and just says airily "Oh you deal with it" then unfortunately you cannot deal with it and there are certain rules which then come into play – called the intestacy rules. In other words, if she doesn't make a Will, there is a state of intestacy. In the case of intestacy, the State has a list of written rules to say what will happen to a person's assets in the event of no Will. Further information on this can be obtained from **www.gov.uk/intestacy** and we will be covering this further in a later chapter.

Suffice to say that intestacy is a situation akin to throwing a rock at a wasp's nest. From the Executor's point of view intestacy is something that they would definitely wish to avoid.

What a Will does is to dispose of all property which the Testator (the deceased) can dispose of in accordance with the Testator's wishes. A Will should also identify all foreseeable events, for example, death of beneficiaries or Executors. It is quite straightforward to make suitable provisions for these eventualities such as putting a clause in 'all children/grandchildren still living at the time of my death....' A Will should also make suitable provisions for children under eighteen, in other words, a guardian may need to be appointed in the event of the Testator dying and the children named in the Will being under eighteen. There may well also need to be a financial provision for this to support the appointed guardian in their duties.

In the first chapter we discussed the responsibilities as Executor with a Will in place for Granny Jones. Let's now imagine a situation where Granny Jones has not actually made a Will. Let's assume therefore that Granny Jones has taken the sensible approach and urged you, as the Executor, to assist her in getting the Will drawn up. She is particularly keen to do this as she has recently been diagnosed with dementia and is now in a nursing home. The three key requirements for a Will to be deemed valid are that there is **capacity, intention** and that the **formalities** of a Will have been followed.

Capacity, Intention, and Formalities

Going through these in turn and in relation to Granny Jones, first of all 'Capacity'. Capacity really means 'does the person have the sufficient mental capacity to understand what it is that they are signing and do they understand who is going to get the assets and what assets they actually have'. This comes back to the well known phrase 'of sound mind'. Just because she has got dementia doesn't necessarily mean she is of unsound mind, as there will be plenty of periods when she is perfectly fine. Your job as the Executor is to make sure that you get this Will drawn up and that would involve visiting her, finding out what it is that she wants doing with all of her assets, making a list of all of those assets and going back and making sure that a Will is drawn up to reflect her intentions.

Once the Will has been drawn up you would then, as the Executor, go back to visit Granny Jones and to have that Will read out to her to make sure that she completely understands it. At this juncture she may point out errors or she may indeed point out changes to be made so bear in mind that there is likely to be another draft. So at that point you would have satisfied yourself that she had the mental capacity to compile a Will and that she understands the **intention** of all that is written in the Will that you have compiled for her. The final stage is to make sure that **formalities** are followed to make sure that this Will is legal and valid. The key points are that she, as the Testator, should sign it and that it should be further signed by two independent witnesses. These witnesses should really not be beneficiaries. This is something that is not well understood as it seems kind and obvious that the beneficiaries should help Granny Jones in getting the Will signed. The reality is that although it may seem to be an act of kindness, a beneficiary's signature on the Will would mean that gifts left to that beneficiary in that Will would become invalid. This would be a rather unfortunate turn of events based simply on a small act of kindness. Obviously a good independent witness would be a medical practitioner but that might not be practical. The witnesses should be signing the Will in front of Granny Jones when **she** signs it and of course it must be dated. One way of avoiding any issues in the future is to make sure that the whole process is videoed. This could certainly help prove, in the event of any arguments, that she did indeed have sufficient mental capacity to draw up the Will as written and that independent witnesses can be shown to be signing the Will.

Wills are often created using professional firms such as probate practitioners or solicitors. One of the advantages of having Wills prepared by a professional firm is that there is a ready supply of independent witnesses.

Revocation

To revoke a Will means that you want to make a previous Will null and void. The process of making a previous Will null and void is called revocation.

It is of course possible that Granny Jones had previously made a Will many years ago and that is somewhere in the bottom of someone's drawer. That Will is now irrelevant as the first thing the new Will says is that any new Will revokes all previous Wills and that would be indicated by the date of the Will. People frequently change their Wills and a Will is not a cumulative set of instructions, the only valid Will is the last Will.

It is however true that the existing Will can be revoked. One particular kind of revocation is where the Testator destroys the Will. Obviously there has to be a clear intention of the Testator wishing to destroy the Will. One recalls the Agatha Christie scenario where the embers of the Will are smouldering in the fireplace and the body of the Testator is lying on the library floor with a knife in the middle of his back. This would tend to indicate that the Testator, Grand Uncle Wilfred, did not intend to revoke his Will and thus 'foul play' was clearly afoot... enter Miss Marple!

Fowl deed

Marriage automatically revokes a Will. So, for instance, had Granny Jones remarried since making her last Will, that last Will would automatically be null and void. This is something that most people, understandably, would not attend to following their happy second nuptials. Having gone through the painful process of making a Will, it would come as a surprise that they would have to make another one once remarried. Interestingly enough, divorce does not actually automatically revoke a Will so had she divorced since the Will, the only aspect of the Will that becomes null and void is the part relating to her 'as was husband'. All the gifts to the husband would become void and would therefore go into the pot of general distributable assets.

It should be noted at this point that the idea of pre-nuptial agreements which are most popular in US soap operas have no validity in the United Kingdom... at the time of writing!

Gifts left by the Testator in the Will

The layout of a standard Will is shown on the next page:

SAMPLE WILL

THIS IS THE LAST WILL AND TESTAMENT of me **EMMA JONES** of 14 Bircham Park (name of town and postcode)

1. **I REVOKE** all former Wills and testamentary dispositions made by me and **DECLARE** this to be my last Will

2. **I APPOINT** the directors of Bradbury Stell Probate Services Limited to be the Executors and Trustees of this my Will and I express the wish that only two of them shall prove my Will and act initially in its trusts

3. **ANY** of my Trustees who is engaged in any profession or business shall be entitled to charge and be paid in priority to all other dispositions contained in this Will or any codicil hereto all professional or business charges for business done by him or any partner or employee of his in connection with the proving or the execution of the trusts hereof including business which an executor or Trustee not being engaged in such profession or business could have done personally

4. **I GIVE** to my brother **MICHAEL JONES** of 27 Field View (name of town and postcode) free of inheritance tax the grandfather clock which I inherited from my father as I know he will take care of it

5. **GIVE** to **VEGANFARM** of The Sanctuary Nr. Lydford Okehampton Devon EX20 4Al (RCN 232208) the sum of Five Thousand Pounds (£5,000) and **I DECLARE** that the written receipt of the treasurer or other competent officer for the time being be a sufficient receipt to my Trustees and if before my death (or after my death but before my Trustees have given effect to the gift) **VEGANFARM** has changed its name changed name or to the body to which the assets have been transferred

6. I give all the rest of my estate not otherwise disposed of by my Will to my Trustees upon trust to pay my debts funeral and testamentary expenses and legacies including all inheritance tax on property passing under my Will and to hold the balance ("my Residuary Estate") on trust for my brother **DAVID JONES** of 15 Barclay Crescent (name of town and postcode) and my said brother **MICHAEL JONES** in equal shares absolutely

IN WITNESS whereof I have hereunto set my hand this   day of   20

SIGNED by the said **EMMA JONES**

as her last Will in the presence
of us both present at the same time who   **STEVE HARLEY**
at her request and in her presence and in
the presence of each other have hereunto
subscribed our names as witnesses   **CHRISTOPHER REBELL**

As can be seen from the standard layout, the first item of gift giving is quite often specific, pecuniary gifts or specific items left to specific people. At the time of writing the Will, Granny Jones may have had in her mind a list of these people that have been good to her or that she wants to be remembered and she will list out various items (in the sample Will above it is a grandfather clock) that she wants left to her brother. The problem with this, of course, is that in a worst case scenario there is not enough money in the person's Estate to cover the pecuniary legacies (as it is much easier to promise money than to actually deliver it!) The gift itself may have been lost or destroyed or replaced or the charity or organisation that is listed in the Will may no longer exist. When this happens these are known as 'failed gifts'.

As already mentioned above, a common 'failed gift' is any gifts left to a spouse prior to a divorce. If there has been a divorce, any gifts to the ex husband or wife would now no longer be valid. This situation also exists where the person to whom the gift was intended has predeceased the Testator (a substitution clause can often alleviate this). In other words, in a situation where Granny Jones, say, intends to leave her grandfather clock to her brother, there are two circumstances where this gift may fail. The grandfather clock may have been broken or destroyed in the period between the creation of the Will and her death, and of course her brother Michael may have died since the Will was drawn up.

In the first instance of the clock being damaged or destroyed, the gift just simply fails outright. There is no provision for a replacement grandfather clock to be given to Michael. It is important to remember that the Will refers to a specific asset. If the asset still survives but Michael does not survive, then the gift passes into the residuary Estate (or to Michael's direct descendants). If a gift fails because the intended recipient has died then the gift will go into the residuary Estate and be distributed according to the instructions in the Will on the residuary Estate.

As the Executor it is your role to advise the Testator as much as possible as to the validity and wisdom of the gifts that she wishes to make. This is not a legal role by any means but it is certainly helpful if you are in front of Granny Jones and she wants to leave a substantial amount of money to a charity that no longer exists. Clearly you would be wise to point that out. If she wants to leave a specific item as a gift to a certain person it is probably wise to make sure that item also still exists.

Sometimes gifts are left to charities and since the Will was written, those charities no longer exist. This is particularly true of local charities that arrive and then die off or are amalgamated into larger charities. If this is the case, as the Executor you will have to do a little bit of homework here and find out what happened to the charity, but you would be correct in executing Granny Jones's wishes by donating that gift to the charity that absorbed the smaller charity.

Another example of a failed gift is where one of the witnesses to the Will was a named recipient in the Will. This provision automatically voids any gifts to that witness, which is why it is really important that the witnesses to a Will be independent and not in any way associated with the Will and, just as in the case of the deceased recipient, these failed gifts will go into the residuary Estate.

The Will should also make mention of what is known as 'the **STEP** provisions'. STEP stands for the Society of Trust and Estate Practitioners and the STEP provisions can be found at **www.STEP.org**. These are a standardised set of provisions and instructions that have been generally agreed upon by the legal profession. Suffice to say at this point that the Will should just mention the STEP provisions and this is a catch-all step to ensure that all eventualities are covered.

It must be remembered that Wills do not need to be registered, they just need to be in existence, and they need to be in existence where someone other than the Testator can find it! Wills can, however, be registered at the Probate Registry and in some instances this can be a good idea.

Bradbury Stell Probate Services Limited will not only prepare Wills but can review Wills that are already in existence.

Pecuniary legacies

Quite often a Will begins with specific pecuniary legacies to be left to specific people. Obviously at the time the Will is written, the Testator will have no idea what the final total of their Estate is going to be. Irrespective of that final total, they may wish to give away specific sums of money to specific relatives or friends.

If there is a specific pecuniary legacy this may well be to a named person or to a charity. This will only take place if there are sufficient funds. If there are insufficient funds in the total Estate to pay out specific pecuniary legacies, then the legacies are distributed in proportion. In broad terms this means that if the final sum of the net Estate (after funeral costs, professional costs and taxes) is less than the sum of the pecuniary legacies then each of the pecuniary legacies is reduced in proportion.

After the pecuniary legacies and specific legacies regarding specific gifts, what is left over is just referred to as 'the residuary' and there will be instructions as to what will happen to that. If the beneficiaries are adults then it is straightforward, but not so straightforward if they are children.

"Anyone who isn't specifically in the will still receives one of these valuable gift bags."

What may often happen is that residual sums will be left in Trust for children until they reach a certain age, e.g. eighteen or twenty-one. What must be avoided is a situation where amounts in the residuary Estate go to beneficiaries that have also predeceased the Testator. To cover this unfortunate eventuality there should be a 'long stop provision'. What this means is that the residue of the Estate should go to, for instance, a charity in the event of the beneficiaries predeceasing.

If money is left to children there should be an age contingency, for example, (£X to be left to Jimmy and Bertie upon their reaching the age of twenty-five). There should also be administrative provisions for the money being held in Trust, i.e. if payments are required for University, Schools, etc.

Letter of Wishes

Appended to the Will there might be a 'Letter of Wishes'.

"His last request was that we close the casket before you begin."

A letter of Wishes is not a legally binding document but it gives useful direction for the Executor particularly in the case of warring siblings! A Letter of Wishes should be as specific as possible but it may say something along the lines of "My youngest nephew Jake has always taken a keen interest in my car collection and I would like him to receive one of those cars after my death".

So this is not a specific legacy to a specific person but more a general intention of what the Testator would like to happen to some of the assets that they had at the point of drawing up the Will. These are merely directions for the Executor based on sentiment and feelings at the time. It must be stressed that a Letter of Wishes is not legally binding.

INTESTACY

A condition of intestacy is that a person is intestate when they have not left a Will. If they have not left a Will, you, as the Executor, of course wouldn't have been named. You might still find yourself being **appointed** as Executor, so you do need to be aware of the intestacy rules.

The intestacy rules were made so that if a person hasn't made a Will, a set of rules can be referred to which have been defined by the state. It is a simple flow chart and takes into account whether the Testator is married and/or has children.

FLOWCHART OUTLINING
THE APPLICATION OF THE INTESTACY RULES

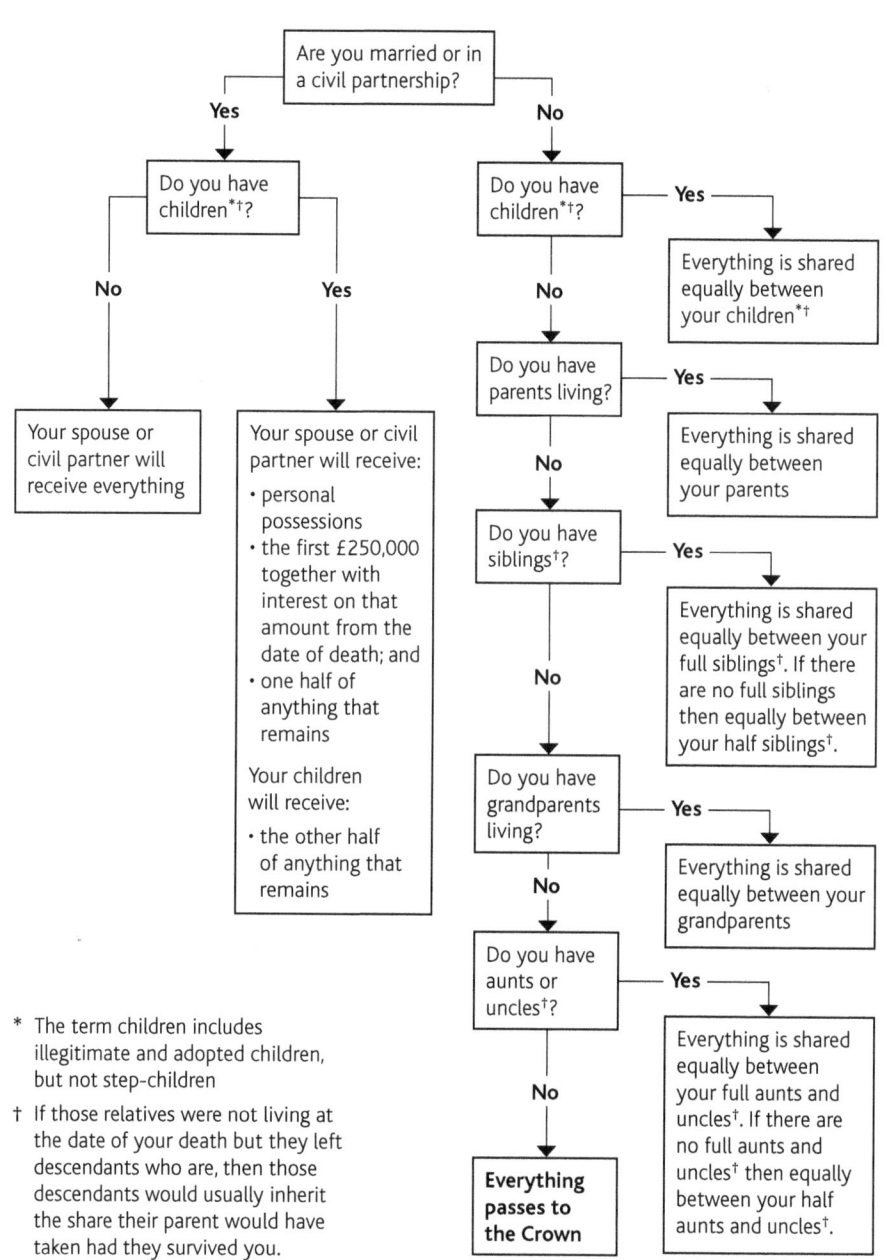

* The term children includes illegitimate and adopted children, but not step-children

† If those relatives were not living at the date of your death but they left descendants who are, then those descendants would usually inherit the share their parent would have taken had they survived you.

If the Testator is not married and has no children, then their assets will pass through a number of relatives and if there are no relatives, sadly they will go back to the state, and **no-one** wants that! The intestacy rules point out the importance of making a Will, and maybe even, controversially, of getting married. A 'partner' or 'significant other' is left nothing whatsoever under the intestacy rules. They may make a claim against the Estate through the courts if they have lived with the deceased for up to two years but all of these things can be avoided by making a Will!

A disappointed potential beneficiary, and a good example of this is a cohabitee, can make a claim to the court but these claims will only succeed if prior to the death that person was maintained by the deceased. This is a good example of where a Letter of Wishes can be important. Granny Jones might decide that she is going to leave nothing whatsoever to her eldest daughter because, well, they haven't spoken for the last twenty years anyway and they never got on. They may never have got on because of a particular incident in the past, whatever that might be. In life these things happen and the Testator can leave her assets to whomever she pleases! It is, however, important that the Letter of Wishes makes this clear. In other words, it would be expected that any direct descendant of the Testator would be left something in the Will. If this didn't happen the Letter of Wishes should make it clear why not. If Granny Jones's eldest daughter had not been maintained by Granny Jones then she will have limited claim on the Estate in any event as she is an adult. A good way round this also is to make sure that Granny Jones leaves the eldest daughter a gift of some sort which will at least leave her feeling less aggrieved and therefore unlikely to make a claim. All such claims must be made within six months of the Grant of Probate in any event.

Claims can be made at:

www.gov.uk/guidance/make-a-claim-to-a-deceased-persons-estate

VALUATION OF ASSETS

Property

Quite often the major part of any individual's Estate is their main residence. Whether it is their main residence or an investment property, the procedure for valuation is the same. The unfortunate news is that as the Executor you have to move fairly promptly after you have been informed of the death. Unlike with shares and bonds whose values are recorded on a day to day basis, a property's value requires the intervention of a valuer. My suggestion is that you speak to three local estate agents (local to where the property is) and ask each of them in turn to meet you at the property, look around the property and write to you with their opinion as to the value of the property. This is the sale value as seen, in other words not the value of the property as it could be or should be but as it was on the day that the agent visited.

"It's doubled in value since the artist was killed by a mastodon."

I'm stating this in clear terms as the reality is that most people who die are old and quite a lot of old people have lived in their properties for a very long time. It is common, therefore, for the property to be somewhat dated and not fitted out with the latest kitchen and bathroom accessories. It is also therefore possible that the walls might need a little bit of painting and decorating, the carpets might be a touch shabby etc etc. Bearing in mind that the value of the property is going to feature on the Inheritance Tax Form and therefore will probably be the major asset responsible for the tax bill, you as the Executor are not in any way incentivised to get that property valued at any more than is absolutely necessary. So tidying it up and giving it a bit of a once-over, which might very well be something you would be inclined to do under normal circumstances, is not to your benefit.

Once the three agents have visited and you have received their valuations, my advice is that you pick an average of those three and put that value in the IHT form. The IHT form is one of a number of forms that need to be completed by you as the Executor – (see later chapter).

It is said that you should also, or instead of Estate Agents, appoint a Chartered Surveyor to perform a thorough and vigorous valuation. In my view it is better to get the opinion of three local estate agents, as they are much closer to the market than one surveyor could be and appointing a surveyor does not necessarily guarantee you a trouble free ride.

A client of mine appointed an RICS qualified surveyor to perform a rigorous valuation shortly after his father died. The surveyor wrote to my client and told him that "in his opinion the value of the property was £1.2 million". The property was in London and this was in 2013 and within a year my client had sold the property for £2.5 million. It was during a time where the market did go a little bit bonkers as tends to happen in London, and my client also spent quite a bit of time and effort tidying up the house between the original valuation and the sale. After assisting my client with the IHT forms, I told him that there was a one in one chance of HMRC investigating this.

"But", my client protested, "I have done all the right things. I have appointed a suitably qualified surveyor, how can it be possible that this could be challenged? It is not reasonable for it to be challenged! I have done my duty", he said, rather crossly.

"Well", I told him, "HMRC are not in existence to be fair or reasonable. They are only in existence to take our money and in this case there is a £1.3 million gap between the valuation and the eventual sale price and HMRC will want as big a slice of that as they can get their hands on".

Suffice to say that my client was challenged by HMRC and did end up in court and did lose. Time machines are unfortunately not available and it is therefore impossible to actually know what the value of this property as submitted on the IHT form should have been. All you can do, as the Executor, is to consult local experts at the time who can give as good an opinion as anyone else as to the likely sale value of the property. (It should be noted that at the time my client was a tax client... and not a probate client!)

With regard to properties, it is also important to check the Land Registry to find out what property the Testator held. It is possible that the Testator would hold a property jointly with someone else and all the deeds are held with that other person and not kept in the bottom of Granny Jones's drawer of 'bits and pieces that might be important in the future'.

This can sometimes happen where a relative (perhaps a grandchild) has been helped to purchase a property in exchange for a percentage of the Deeds. So let's say Granny Jones gave favourite granddaughter £30,000 but decided that she would also retain a slice of said property. She may have put herself on the Deeds as being a 10% owner. It is quite likely that she would not have kept any documentary evidence of this but as a 10% owner of a property that has since substantially risen in value, this will form part of Granny Jones's Estate. In other words, it has to be known and the last resort is the Land Registry which will have details of all properties that Granny Jones has any entitlement to.

Details of any land ownership can be checked at the Land Registry or by checking with Granny Jones's conveyancer. Checking at the Land Registry can be done at:

www.onlinelandregistry.org.uk

Chattels

The title of this book is 'Where There's a Will, There's a Relative' which is a rather comic Yorkshire expression of mistrust with regard to the behaviour of members of your dearly beloved family, particularly where money is concerned. However, it is actually in the case of chattels where most problems will normally arise. All the major assets in the Estate can be valued independently and as the Executor it is your job to deal with this and to turn these assets into cash. You may have been given instructions as to how to dispose of paintings and jewellery but I'm afraid these will still need to be valued. Auctioneers are only too willing to give you a value of furniture, art and jewellery that should be in the house, and if there are more than one auctioneer available locally to visit the premises, I would definitely recommend getting two such valuations. They are likely to be a little bit less cooperative than estate agents but there are incentives for them as you may appoint them at a future date to sell some of the assets.

The likelihood is, though, that most of the chattels in the house will be divided up as you see fit. In other words, the Testator will leave you no clear instructions as to what to do with them but merely to divide it up amongst members of the family. This probably won't be the case for the more valuable chattels, for example, jewellery. These are the situations where a distant cousin will suddenly emerge from the woodwork and say something along the lines of "Well your mother always wanted me to have that ring and told me so frequently" and this is despite the fact that you have specific instructions as the Executor to give all the jewellery to a nominated daughter or daughters.

One client of mine, as the Executor, decided to take matters into his own hands and the third weekend after the death of his relative spent a whole two days cataloguing every single item in each of the rooms to come up with a list ten A4 pages long with twenty items on each page. He then invited all the beneficiaries to sit round a table and they each in turn chose an item from the list. Those items that were not chosen were disposed of or given to a local charity shop. In this way, my client was able to avoid any family conflict over the less valuable, but often more sentimental items, which cause the most trouble.

WHAT IS AN ESTATE AND WHAT IS IN IT?

As previously mentioned, the 'Estate' is literally a full compilation of all the assets that the Testator held at the time of death. This could be property held in the Testator's name, alone or jointly.

Property and land held by the Testator is either in **sole ownership,** held as a **joint tenant** or held as **tenants in common.**

Tenants in Common vs Joint Tenants

If the property and land is held as **sole ownership** then all of that property passes into the Estate. Property held as **joint tenants** (this also includes joint bank accounts and actually despite its name has nothing to do with a property tenancy) will automatically pass to the surviving party of the joint tenancy. So in other words, if a house is held as joint tenants between husband and wife and the wife dies, the property automatically passes to the husband and does not form part of the wife's Estate. This is also true of joint bank accounts. If the husband dies all the money in the joint bank account will go automatically to the wife and does not form part of the Estate.

This is entirely different with **tenants in common.** You will more often than not see properties conveyed to couples as being held as tenants in common. When conveyancers (normally a solicitor) carry out property transactions they normally talk to couples about this and make sure that their property is held as tenants in common. This means that in the event of one of their deaths, if the property is held between the two as tenants in common the deceased's part will go into **their** Estate and the remainder will obviously remain with the surviving partner.

As an Executor the only aspect of the above provisions that will become really important is where bank accounts are held jointly. Let's imagine a situation with Granny Jones where Mr Jones was still alive and they held a considerable amount of money in a joint bank account. This would mean that the husband could automatically get rights to that bank account without having to wait for the probate to be granted. (see Grant of Probate in later chapter) If you are unaware as to whether the property is held as joint tenants or tenants in common, you may need to use the facilities at the Land Registry and to search for the property or refer to the conveyancer who was in charge of the property transaction when it happened.

Pensions

A pension itself does not normally form part of an Estate if the Testator had a final salary scheme type pension. In these types of pensions, the pensioner is paid a certain amount per month and that amount is worked out by the pension provider. The conditions of this are that once the pensioner dies, the pension will automatically cease. There may, however, be a death in service payment. This is unlikely to apply to Granny Jones as she is aged 92, but it is worthwhile checking! Certainly if the Testator was still working when they died then there may well be a death in service payment applicable and you as the Executor need to find out whether that provision applies. Being the nominated Executor does mean that you will be able to open up a conversation with any pension providers named by the Testator. Quite often death in service payments are outside of the Estate as they will be paid to a nominated beneficiary, however, the homework on the part of the Executor is to contact the pension company and find out whether there is any death in service payments payable to the Estate or payable to nominated beneficiaries.

The most common type of pension, however, is a defined contribution style of pension where you literally have a 'pot of money' or investments sitting in the pension fund. There will be provisions in the pension to detail what happens to that pot of money but it may well pass to the Estate and again, as the Executor, you must contact the pension company to find out if that was the case. This will probably be the most troublesome item of your duties as an Executor. Pension companies are almost as slow as HMRC in responding and you will have a number of detailed questions to ask them. Do not be surprised if some of the institutions that you write to do not respond promptly, so keep a log of when you wrote to them and how they responded. Some of the institutions you write to will definitely need to be harassed in a polite and firm manner!

Insurance Policies

Life insurance policies are policies which will pay out upon a person's death. Quite often life insurance does not pay out after a certain age but if the insured is below that age, the amount paid out would form part of the Estate. As the Executor you should certainly make sure you find out whether there is a life insurance policy that is still in existence.

Life insurance policies are sometimes 'written into Trust'. What that means is that upon the death, the insurance will pay out to the Trust and that will also be outside of the Estate and not pass to the Estate. This is because a Trust is a separate legal entity to the Testator. What the Executor should do in these situations is to send a death certificate to the insurance company and they will release the funds automatically to the Trust. It is then the responsibility of the Trustees to administer those funds. If the life insurance policy is not written into Trust then the proceeds of the policy will need to form part of the Estate.

INHERITANCE TAX

Inheritance Tax used to be called Estate Tax and was mainly introduced after the Second World War with the creation of the Welfare State. Prior to that it was very easy for wealthy families to leave all of their money to their progeny. Following the second World War the government saw an excellent opportunity to extract larger sums of money from the landed gentry and other rich people to finance their brand new project, The National Health Service. Since then it has become an accepted part of the tax landscape but people have over the years invented all kinds of ruses and schemes to escape the tax. The government has clamped down on many of these but there are still a number of very efficacious give-aways that should definitely be taken advantage of.

"For those with particularly ungrateful children,
the inheritance tax can be a comfort."

There are three main occasions where inheritance tax may be charged. One obviously is on death, another one is on a potentially exempt transfer (a PET) and the other one is on a lifetime gift into Trust.

PETs (Potentially Exempt Transfer)

Dealing with PETs first, a PET is a gift or gifts made in the seven years prior to death. Any gifts made outside of that period are entirely free of inheritance tax but within that seven year period tax is potentially levied and it is levied on a sliding scale – in other words if the gift was made six years prior to death then the percentage of that gift that goes back into the Estate is quite small but if it is one year from death, then the gift becomes fully added back into the Estate. These provisions are to obviously stop people avoiding inheritance tax by giving it all away as soon as they know that they are terminally ill. HMRC don't like the idea of anyone getting away without paying tax on their money even if they are close to death! It is very important throughout the lifetime to document PETs particularly if they are significant. There is an annual gift allowance of £3000 which is exempt from IHT and this can be carried over for one year. This means effectively that in the event of a carry-over of an unused gift allowance, £6000 could be transferred as a gift on 5 April to one person and £3000 the next day to the same person (as 6 April is the start of the new tax year) so over those two days, a significant amount can be transferred and that would be exempt from IHT. This can often be the most troublesome part of an Executor's duties. Granny Jones has been particularly prodigious in her gift giving over the last five years and she may or may not have documented all of those gifts. Sadly it may well be a case of trawling through chequebook stubs or bank statements to find out who she has given money away to. This is not an easy task.

It must also be noted that IHT can be charged on **joint property** (see previous chapter 'definition of joint property') so that the amount chargeable to IHT might be different to the probate value (amounts held jointly do not form part of the Estate, but confusingly form part of what is taxable). This is obviously to prevent people putting all their money in a joint account with their brother, son, significant other and having that amount pass to the surviving person in the joint agreement (joint tenants) and avoiding any IHT on it! God Bless the HMRC .....

The IHT on lifetime gifts into Trusts (Trusts are dealt with in more detail in a later chapter) is 20% and the main rate is 40%, the reduced rate of 36% applies where 10% of the total Estate is left to charity. All gifts to charity throughout the lifetime of the deceased are obviously exempt from IHT, as are all gifts to spouses.

The nil rate band is an amount which is free of IHT and at the time of writing that amount is £325,000 for any individual. The individual may also inherit the nil rate band from their spouse. This is very common. Granny Jones may have recently died but her husband died ten years previously and because he left all of his Estate to his wife, none of the nil rate band was used and therefore she now has two nil rate bands to utilise on her death and that is two times £325,000 equalling £650,000.

There is also now an allowance called the Residence Nil Rate Band (RNRB). The residence needs to be a qualifying residence (normally just a family home rather than a commercial property) and it needs to be inherited closely 'i.e. normally left to the children or siblings who inherit the property to live in or to live in and dispose of later'. The current rate for RNRB is £125,000 but this will rise to £175,000 by the tax year 20/21. The Residence Nil Rate Band is fully available up to an Estate size of £2 million but after that it tapers off quite sharply. The RNRB is also passed on from the deceased's spouse. This means that Granny Jones not only gets Mr Jones's nil rate band but also his Residence Nil Rate Band, meaning that the tax free part of the Estate could be as much as £1million.

Interest is charged on IHT not paid within six months of the death of the Testator and the IHT forms themselves must be returned within twelve months of the death. The Executors are personally liable for the return of the form and will be fined personally if the form is not submitted! Who would be an Executor? IHT is payable in instalments for certain parts of the IHT e.g. land and buildings, some shares, agricultural land.

The ultimate Catch 22 about inheritance tax is that the Grant of Probate cannot happen until the IHT is paid and quite often the IHT cannot be paid until some of the assets are sold. This is particularly true, of course, when the major asset is the family home.

With regard to our fictitious Executor and his Granny Jones, he would be well advised to talk to her on appointment about making sure that sufficient bank and cash reserves are available to pay the IHT so that he or she can obtain the Grant of Probate. It must also be added that HMRC will allow a time to pay arrangement if the major asset to be sold to pay the tax is the family home.

Assets Exempt From Inheritance Tax - Business Property Relief

Shares held in an unquoted company (e.g. a family company) left to children of the deceased are usually left outside the taxable Estate. In other words, Business Property Relief (BPR) is where shares in unquoted companies or shares in a sole trader organisation are passed through the Testator's Estate. These are exempt from IHT, but there are restrictions on this. The restrictions are that the business must have existed for two years and it must **not** have traded or dealt with land, building, securities or investments.

The most tax advantageous way of making this kind of bequest is that it should be left to beneficiaries **other** than the spouse. Business Property Relief also applies to business premises. Let us imagine a situation where our fictitious Testator, Granny Jones, also inherited a business from her husband when he died. When she dies, even though she does not have any executive responsibility for it, she can pass the shares on to her children entirely free of IHT even though the assets are within the Estate.

To contrast with an earlier point where IHT is payable even though an asset is outside of the Estate (e.g. a joint account), this is in fact the exact opposite. Although the asset of the business forms part of the Estate, it is not chargeable to IHT.

TRUSTS

"I don't fetch. I have a trust fund."

There are all kinds of different Trusts that can or have been set up. Trusts were in fact invented in the Middle Ages during the Crusades. The 'Trust' was in fact a trusted friend who held on to land on behalf of the Crusader just in case he didn't come back! There are three parties to a Trust – the Settlor, the Trustee and the Beneficiary. The Settlor is the person who has to set up the Trust. This Trust is to be settled upon a defined list of beneficiaries after the Settlor has passed away. The Beneficiaries are obviously the people who benefit from that Trust and the Trustee or Trustees are the people who manage the Trust on behalf of the beneficiaries.

There are various different types of Trust, e.g. 'life interest Trust', 'discretionary Trust', 'bereaved minor Trust', 'eighteen to twenty-five Trust'. There are others but these are the main ones that are usually used. Trusts may have a practical use and an example of this is the life interest Trust which protects a wife's house for the period she is alive but which then passes on the death of the wife to the children. One of the things that this ensures is that the children will eventually get the property **but** she can't pass it on to a new partner. The wife in effect becomes a life tenant of the property. This kind of Trust is often used with second marriages, where the children are from a first marriage.

Another type of Trust is the most common type of Trust and that is a discretionary Trust where the distribution of the Trust to the beneficiaries is entirely at the discretion of the Trustee. As the Executor you may even find yourself being a Trustee. A Trustee is obviously a trusted individual who can use a defined asset for the benefit of a defined beneficiary. It is not a responsibility to be taken lightly!

New laws were introduced in 2006 that made Trusts a lot less attractive. It meant that inheritance tax can actually be charged on the creation of a Trust at 20% (although the nil rate band is taken into account). So, for example, if a Trust was created for £400,000, 20% would be payable immediately to HMRC on its creation. That 20% would be £400,000 less the nil rate band so in other words £75,000 times 20%, i.e. £15,000. The IHT is also paid by the Settlor, which effectively means that IHT is paid in advance of the Settlor's death! This, unsurprisingly, is a somewhat bitter pill to swallow.

Trusts made up for disabled children or bereaved minors are exempt from IHT and Trusts made out for those aged 18-25 are also treated favourably by HMRC.

OBTAINING THE PROBATE
(Grant of Representation)

As the Executor you need to know that the bulk of Granny Jones's Estate cannot be turned into cash until you have obtained the Grant of Probate. This is literally a certificate that grants you as the Personal Representative of Granny Jones the right, on presentation of the certificate to the asset holder, to liquidate that asset into cash.

In common with much of the law regarding probate, there are a number of words for the same thing so the Grant of Representation is also another word for the Grant of Probate.

The Grant of Probate gives the Personal Representatives (the PRs) the authority to deal with the Estate. There are certain items of the Estate that do not require the Grant of Probate to be granted in order to distribute them and these are –

- Chattels
- Cash
- Small amounts in bank accounts, i.e. those amounts less than £5000 can be released without a grant, just with a death certificate

Where the property is held jointly (not just property but actual bank accounts) a death certificate is all that is required to pass property on to the joint holder.

In order to apply for the Grant of Representation, five things are sent along to the Probate Office –

- Form PA1
- Form IHT 421 and IHT 205
- The Will
- Court Fees
- A Statement of Truth

An example of the Statement of Truth is included in the probate form PA1 and the link for this is **www.gov.uk/PA1P**. IHT Forms can also be obtained here. It should be noted that Form IHT 421 may not be required if the Estate is small, i.e. it is beneath the nil rate band of £325,000. The actual size of the Estate is summarised in Form IHT 205. If the Estate is over £325,000 then Form IHT 400 has to be completed and that has many many supplementary forms for each different kind of asset. To apply for an IHT reference, Form IHT 422 needs to be completed and this can also be found on the government website:

www.gov.uk/government/publications/inheritance-tax-application-for-an-inheritance-tax-reference-IHT422

All inheritance forms now can be submitted online rather than sent in by paper. This is a new service provided from 2020.

Once the Grant of Probate has been obtained, a stamped copy of the Grant needs to be sent to each asset holder. It is important, therefore, when applying for the Grant that enough stamped copies are obtained. As a rough guide, one for each different kind of asset plus five spares is a decent number to aim for. The asset holder might be a bank or an investment management firm or a wealth management firm or a unit trust etc etc. It might even be an estate agent. The asset holder needs to be instructed to liquidate the holdings and send the money directly to a named account. This named account should be an executor account and as the Executor you should have made sure this was set up as soon as you are notified of the Testator's death. It is, unsurprisingly, a difficult job as it requires communication with banks. There are some banks that specialise in executor accounts but most of them will look at you as if you had three heads as soon as you mention the word 'executor'. It is a trying process but necessary as when you eventually draw up the Estate accounts, it is much better for you if all the income and outgoings are in one place.

SETTLING THE ESTATE

Having obtained the Grant of Probate and sent off the certificates to the various asset holders, money will start to come into the executor account. At this point some debts may need to be settled and these are settled in the following order:-

1. Funeral/wake expenses
2. HMRC – non IHT
3. Any costs related to collecting and preserving assets
4. Any professional fees or probate registry fees
5. IHT

Of course it is possible that someone else may have paid for the funeral (because funerals are events that cannot be put off by financial considerations!). In this case that person can be paid directly out of the executor account.

It also must be noted that Capital Gains Tax might be payable by the Estate if the sale price of an asset is much in excess of the value of the asset stated in the probate application.

If it is found that the Estate is insolvent, i.e. the debts of the Testator exceed the assets then the debts must be settled in accordance with the above list. In other words funeral expenses would be settled first and IHT would be settled last.

It must be noted that if it is likely that once a beneficiary knows that they are a beneficiary, they will be keen to get their hands on the cash as soon as they possibly can. It must be stressed that the Executor must not be tempted to distribute any of the Estate before the Section 27 period has lapsed. A Section 27 Notice is an advertisement that the personal representative of an Estate places in the London Gazette and a local newspaper to inform any potential creditors that the Estate is soon going to be distributed. The Section 27 Notice period is normally between two and three months. That Notice period would be mentioned in the advertisement. Executors will ordinarily have a period of twelve months from the date of death before beneficiaries can reasonably get agitated.

Deed of Variation

A Deed of Variation is something that rearranges the disposition of the property from the Estate by the beneficiary themselves (rather than Testator). In other words, the beneficiary might decide themselves to make a change to how much they are actually going to take from the Estate. This might be the case where the beneficiary believes that it is more tax efficient to, say for instance, distribute to charities or to children. A Deed of Variation needs to be drawn up before final distribution is made. If the property or assets are passed to a new beneficiary from the original beneficiary then this is treated as a PET (potentially exempt transfer) to the new beneficiary. Because gifts to charities are exempt from IHT, if a beneficiary decides that a particular charity can get an extra slice of money instead of them, then it will lead to less IHT being paid. The timing of the drawing up of the Deed of Variation is prior to the final Estate accounts. So in other words, this is an event that can take place any time between the death and the drawing up of the final accounts. It may appear that this is an act that contradicts the Will of the Testator. However, clearly it is up to the beneficiaries themselves to decide whether or not they wish to accept the funds and whether they want to distribute them differently. It is quite often more tax efficient to have the distribution performed differently and a beneficiary may decide to do so particularly in consideration of the fact that their own children would stand to benefit from the money eventually in any event.

Finalising Tax Position

Before finally distributing the residuary Estate to the beneficiaries, the Executor must finalise the tax position. It is almost certainly going to be the case that the final values realised for all of the assets will be different from values of those assets submitted to HMRC in the original IHT forms. It may well be that less was realised than anticipated or more. Once HMRC are satisfied that the correct amount of IHT has been paid, they will issue what is known as an IHT 300 and that is basically a certificate to clear the Executor of all further responsibilities to HMRC essentially letting the Executor off the hook!

"When I die, please cremate me and send my ashes to the tax office. Write on the envelope, NOW YOU HAVE EVERYTHING"

When distributing the Estate the Executor needs to make sure that he has proof of receipt from all beneficiaries to say that their bequest has been settled. This is as much the case for relatives of the deceased as it is for charities. One thing the Executor must always take into account is that as a PR the Executor is personally liable for any errors or omissions made.

Unknown Creditors and Beneficiaries

There are some steps that Executors can take to protect themselves against the unknowns, e.g. unknown creditors. The Executor can put an ad in the London Gazette and a local paper to announce the death of the Testator and to ask for anyone to come forward who feels that they might be a beneficiary in the Estate.

Final Jobs

The other jobs to make sure are completed are that there will be a final Tax Return for the deceased in the year of death and CGT may be payable by the Estate if the assets held during the administration period exceeded the Probate value and were then sold by the Estate. If assets are passed to beneficiaries in whole, then sold by the beneficiaries themselves, i.e. after the administration period, the beneficiaries may also be personally liable to Capital Gains Tax.

"Not much in the way of hard assets, I'm afraid, but he did leave some highly desirable organs."

A set of Estate accounts should be drawn up for the benefit of the beneficiaries. There is no prescribed format for this, in other words an Excel sheet is absolutely fine but it must show the following –

1. Statement of the provisions of the Will
2. A capital account to show the value of the assets at death
3. The value realised
4. Statement of liabilities and expenses

As a PR it must be noted that the Executor, despite being under a lot of pressure from a lot of people, is not legally bound to distribute the Estate before the end of one year.

An example of a final set of accounts is shown on the next page.

SCHEDULE OF ASSETS AND LIABILITIES

	£
Freehold Property (in her sole name)	
14 Bircham Park	350,000
Bank and Building Society Accounts	
Lloyds Bank Current Account No: 25467667	14,754
Principality Building Society Account No: 45786	69,523
Investments	
Quoted shares (no controlling interest)	47,004
Unquoted shares: 650 Atherton Trading Limited £1 ord. (25% holding). - owned for 15 years	70,000
Pension Arrears	
State pension	226
Life Assurance	
Stellar Assurance Co. Ltd Policy No. 67453	
- Proceeds payable to Emma's Estate	40,000
Personal Possessions	
Cash (in house)	65
Furniture	
Jewellery	2,300
Car	8,700
Debts	
K. Richards & Sons Funeral Directors	3,700
Utility bills	65

Once the accounts are drawn up, it is a good idea to have the beneficiaries sign the accounts to make sure that they have understood them.

When that is done and the beneficiaries have been paid out, then the Executor's work is complete... as is this book!